WHO TO MARRY

MAKE A RIGHT CHOICE IN ORDER TO DWELL IN HAPPINESS AND TRANQUILITY

ADAM D. ASSABURY

ISBN: 9798371631985

DEDICATION

This book is dedicated to my beloved late mother in person of Maryam Galadima, and to my lovely family members, my lovely sister Khadija Danladi who supported me in one way or the other to undergo this work

CONTENTS

APPRECIATION

All thanks and praises be to Almighty Allah the Lord of the universe and may the peace and blessings of ALLAH be upon our beloved Prophet Muhammad (SAW), his household, his companions and as well as those that follow the guardians till the day of judgment. I thank Allah for given me the strength, sound mind, good health and wisdom to carry out this work. My gratitude goes to Dr. Islamil Salahudeen for his immense assistance offered to me during the period of this work. I am also grateful to my siblings for their support rendered to me.

JAZAKUMULLAHUKHAIR.

CHAPTER ONE

Introduction

Marriage is the relationship between man and woman who are husband and wife. In other words, marriage is a relationship that exists between a man (husband) and a woman (wife) with aim of creating a harmonious life for themselves. Marriage is an act of worship. In Qur'an ALLAH says; And among His signs is this, that He created for you wives from among yourselves, that you may find repose in them, and He has put between you affection and mercy. Verily, in that are indeed signs for a people who reflect. (Qur30:21). Prophet Muhammad (SAW) said; when someone marry he has complete half of his religion (deen). We all believed that is natural for men having emotional feelings for women, likewise women too. ALLAH says: beautified for men is the love of things they covet; women, children, much of gold and silver (wealth), branded beautiful horses, cattle and well-tilled land. This is the pleasure of present world's life; but with Allah has the excellent return (paradise) with him. (Qur3:14). The only way for them to express or satisfied their emotional feelings legally and also raise a legitimate progeny is only by contract which is known as marriage. Marriage is essential in life, is the only legal way that one can vent out his sexual desire. Marriage serves as a security guard to spouses from transgression (committing illicit sexual intercourse). And marriage is a joyous unionship and also brings happiness in one's life. Prophet Muhammad (SAW) said; in this dunya (world) there is little enjoyment and the enjoyment of it, is righteous wife. Yes, there is no doubt in this hadith that the enjoyment of this world is being blessed with righteous wife, because is the only way to have repose in your life. When you are rich and have a lot of wealth and you are been afflicted with bad wife, the happiness will not be there in your home and your life as well due to her bad attitude or bad character. As we can see from aforementioned verse and hadith above, ALLAH created wives for us in order to have repose in them, and also to dwell in happiness and joy. The question someone might ask is that, are the all married men and women (spouses) having the repose that ALLAH mentioned from the above verse (ayat)..? Nowadays, we have heard about marriage been failed, matrimonial homes been broken, and spouses living like a cats and dogs. Majority of the spouses are not living in harmony, why because they failed to follow the right steps when selecting their life partner (spouses). This book WHO TO MARRY is going to figure out or provide some profound qualities from QUR'AN and HADITHS of (SAW) which one should sought in a spouse in order to choose or select a right spouse, because we do make deadly mistake when selecting a spouse without considering those qualities which result to broken of matrimonial homes today. I will try my best to elaborate on those qualities that should be sought in a life partner IN SHA ALLAH. Furthermore, I will also provide some profound qualities which I term as fundamental pillars of love which is expected both husband and wife should all possess in their dictionaries. And we are going to discuss duties of spouses in their matrimonial home in order to dwell in happiness and repose (security in love or relationship) and also build a solid and vibrant matrimonial home which is free from intruders.

CHAPTER TWO

FEATURES OF A GOOD SPOUSE

In this chapter we will discuss qualities that should be sought in a spouse and I will like to separate the features or qualities that should be sought in a spouse.

QUALITIES OF A GOOD WIFE

Features of a good wife are the good qualities that a woman possesses or that she is being endowed with and which make her relationship with her husband last longer and also dwell in happiness. Therefore, these qualities or features should be sought when selecting a life partner (wife), in order to have repose in your life.

1. Righteousness

The first essential quality of a good wife is righteousness. Righteousness is a piety that someone attained by strictly following the doctrines of the religion without compromise and with the aim of seeking the pleasure of his/her creator (ALLAH).

Prophet Muhammad (SAW) said; a woman is married for four things, her wealth, her family status, her beauty and her religion. So you should take possession of (marry) the religion woman otherwise, you will be a loser (Sahih Al-Bukhari).Righteous wife is a wife that has GOD fearing (taqwa).

Benefits of marrying a Righteous wife

I. She will always assist you in the affairs of your life (dunya) and religion (hereafter) too.
II. She will also make sure that your children are raised in a religious way.
III. She will not engage herself into dreadful sins because she has (taqwa) God fearing.

Therefore, righteousness must be sought when selecting a wife and it shouldn't be compromise.

2. Good character

Sometimes good character and righteousness are often misunderstood by the seekers of wives, some thinks that if a woman is religious (righteous), she is qualified to be choosing or selected as a wife without considering her character. She will only be certified to become a wife provided she has a good character. Good character is a behavior which is acceptable in a society. Good character is one of the qualities that must be sought when selecting a wife.

Features of good character are: respect, sympathy, honest, humility, kindness, decent, obedient, generous, friendly, mercy.

Therefore, a woman without the above qualities should not be selected as a wife even though she has the Islamic knowledge. Because Prophet Muhammad (SAW) said; there are three individuals that when they supplicate to ALLAH, their supplication will not be answered. A man who has a wife of bad character that lack manners but he does not divorce her, a man who lends money to another person without taking witnesses, lastly, a man who gives money to a weak minded person. The hadith mentioned above, show us the danger of marrying a woman that has bad character. Sometimes you will see lady with Islamic knowledge but having bad character. Therefore, this kind of girls should be avoided and you should marry a lady that is righteous and has a good character.

3. Shyness

Shyness is another essential quality that should be sought when selecting a wife. Prophet Muhammad (SAW) said; shyness is a branch of faith (Iman).Therefore, this quality shouldn't be taking for granted because any woman that lacks this quality, she can misbehave at any time. Shyness serves as a moderator of behavior of any human being. So marry a woman that has this golden quality because it has great impact in her character or attitude.

4. Loving

One should marry a woman that possess loving and caring attitude. Love is what keeps a relationship tight and happily, to determine whether a woman has a loving attitude one's has to look at her family, most especially her mum does she possess loving attitude toward her family. Prophet Muhammad (SAW) said; marry a woman who loves and can bear many children, because I will boast of your numbers in the Day of Judgment (Abu Dawud and an-Nasa'i). Love is the life of any relationship most especially marriage because if love is lost in any relationship, automatically the relationship or the marriage will be like a hell.

5. Contentment

Contentment is another vital quality that one should sought when selecting a life partner. Contentment is a state of being happy and satisfied with what you have without complaining. Marriage do failed, because some women lacks heart contented, they keep on nagging, complaining with what is been given to them. They think what is given to them will not suffice them; some women even push their husbands to do something that is illicit in order to satisfied their heart desire. All their thought is that managing the little resource or wealth that their husbands possess is a disgrace to them.

Therefore, contentment is easily found in a virgin then matron, because Prophet Muhammad (SAW) said; "marry virgin, because they have fertile womb, sweeter speech, less slyness and easily satisfied with little wealth" (at-Tabarani).

It is easier for a virgin to be satisfied with little wealth that her husband possesses than matron because of her level of exposure. Therefore men should avoid women that lack this quality.

6. Virgin

Is a young woman, who has never had a sex in her life, virginity is not a compulsory condition when selecting a wife because some women lost their virginity in an accident, but marrying a virgin is recommended. In the hadith of Jabir, he was asked by Prophet Muhammad (SAW) have you married, O Jabir. He replied "yes" and He asked him (SAW), is she a virgin or non- virgin? He replied non virgin. Prophet (SAW) then said; why didn't you marry a virgin who will play with you and you with her and she will laugh with you and you with her... (Sahih al-Bukhari and Muslim). We observed from the above hadith that marrying a virgin is a recommendable quality one should sought in marriage.

Importance of marrying a virgin

i. Easily satisfied with little wealth
ii. They have fertile womb
iii. Less slyness
iv. They have sweeter speech
v. Above all you will be the first person to graze in her green pasture, unlike a matron that has been grazed by another person before passing to you.

7. Compatibility

Compatibility is essential quality one should consider when selecting a wife. You have to check is she compatible to you and you to her.
Prophet Muhammad (SAW) said; "make a good choice for your seed, marry women who are compatible to you, and marry your daughters to them who are compatible" (ibn majah and al-Hakim).
Major features of compatibility in marriage are; compatibility in religion and character, you have to make sure that her religion background and character is compatible to yours. These major features of compatibility should not be taken for granted because it has great impact in your relationship. Other features of compatibility that should not be considered mandatory are; age, financial status and family status but is essential to know that age plays vital role in marriage. If the spouse observed that, the age will affect one of them to fulfill his/her duty upon his/her partner. Advisably, is better for them to avoid such kind of marriage contract because one of them will be cheated due to inability of the second party to fulfill his/her duty.

8. Patience

Patience is the ability to continue doing something that is difficult and time taken without becoming upset or fed-up. Patience is also persistence and perseveres. Patience is one of the greatest qualities one should sought when selecting a life partner.

Almighty Allah says in Qur'an that, He is with those that exercise patient. A women that lack this quality, (patience), her matrimonial home always be like a hell, because her impatience and aggressive attitude.

You will agree with me that a woman that possesses this essential quality (patience), you hardly see or hear her quarrelling or fighting with her husband. If she is annoyed or facing some challenges in her matrimonial home, she will perseveres and exercise patient and no one will know the secret and lapses of her matrimonial home. Unlike a lady with impatient attitude all the difficulties and lapses of her husband will be broadcasted or televise to the world. Happiness and joy is yours when you marry a lady that has patience in her dictionary.

9. Naïve

A naive is someone that has less experience in life. This quality should be sought when selecting a wife. A girl that is naive is simple, easy to control, easy to rule, tent to trust people easily and easily believe things without raising a query unlike a lady that is not a naive. This quality is easily present in a virgin than matron, or a young girl that is in between 14-17 years old.

10. Hard working

Hardworking is another vital quality that every person should sought when selecting a spouse. A hardworking girl always put more effort to make sure that she discharges her duties by performance in her matrimonial home, a hardworking girl always tidy her home, make sure that everywhere is clean and tidy and always put more effort in maintaining her husband. Unlike, a lazy type, which doesn't have time for her husband and always leave her matrimonial home untidy and unclean due to her lazy attitude. Love and affection do increase when you marry a girl that she's hardworking type.

11. **Child bearing**

We all know that one of the purposes of marriage is to give birth to off springs. It is recommended to marry a young girl who will bear many children. Because Prophet Muhammad (SAW) said; "marry a woman who is loving and can bear many children because I will boast of your number (multitude) on the Day of Judgment (Abu-Dawud and bn Nasa'i)"

The importance or benefits of marrying a woman that will procreate are:

i. You follow the Sunnah of (S.A.W) because he said, marry a bearer of many children, because I will boast of your number on the day reckoning.
ii. Because children are the adornment of the life of this world (Qur'an 18:46).
iii. Prophet Muhammad (S.A.W) Said; when someone died, all his affairs in this world (Dunya) are terminated unless three things. (i) The re-occurring charity (ii) the knowledge that is beneficial (iii) the righteous child that always pray for his parents.
iv. Children are helpers to their parents
v. Your name will always be mentioned when you have a child even though you are dead.
vi. Given birth to young ones, is the only way to maintain the existence of human beings in this world (Dunya).

If every person in this world should decide that they are not going to reproduce or procreate again, one day, this world will be empty without humans because the existing ones are dead.

12. Indoor type
Indoor types are category of people that doesn't like going outside unnecessarily; they prefer staying inside their houses. Indoor type is a recommended quality one should sought when selecting a life partner. Allah says stay in your houses and do not display yourselves like that of the time of ignorance… (Qur' 33:33). This is the command of Allah upon women that they should stay in their homes. And the benefit for marrying a girl that has this quality is that, she will always have ample time for her husband. She will gain more ground in her husband heart, because she has enough time to take care of her husband.

13. Educated
Educated person is someone that has knowledge; education is essential quality that is recommended to be sought when choosing a life partner. Knowledge can be categorized into two;
(i) Islamic knowledge and

(ii) Western knowledge

All these knowledge are essential for women to acquire them, most especially, Islamic knowledge because her progeny will be the beneficiary of it and she will be able to know how to worship her creator and also solve some problems related to Islamic aspect.

A wise woman that is educated always uses her knowledge that she acquired to construct a solid love in her husband heart and also used that knowledge to lead her matrimonial home in a positive direction

14. Her family reputation

It is very important to also consider her family reputation when selecting a wife. Because when you marry a woman that came from bad family, surely there will be a negative influence on your wife character or her attitude. It's recommended to marry a woman that come from good family, because her family do help in solving some problems in matrimonial home. Prosperity is yours when you follow the advice of the wise men.

15. **Beauty**

When a girl is good looking and prepossessing, we says she is beautiful. I decided to bring this quality last in this chapter in order to show the less important of it when selecting a life partner (wife). This is where most men make a lot of harmful and deadly mistake in their life when selecting a wife. The majority go for beautiful ones without considering other qualities that I mentioned above. That is why, some marriage has failed, and matrimonial home has being broken and physical assault is increasing, children being raised in a way that is not in accordance with Islamic teachings. The repose that Allah says you may find in her will not be there, and also a wife and husband living like a cat and Dog. Because they failed to abide by the admonition given by the Prophet Muhammad (SAW) which says; marry a woman that has deen (Righteous). The purpose of this advice is for us to dwell in happiness and joy. I am not saying that if you want to marry a woman don't marry a beautiful one, behold, what I am saying here is that don't compromise righteousness (Deen), good character with beautiful. If a woman is beautiful but she is not righteous (Religion), she doesn't deserve to be selected as a wife. .Beauty is a focal point which creates or hatches seeds of love in the heart but what really make or facilitate the growth of those seeds of love and make them live in the heart forever, is righteousness and good character. Beauty can fade but righteousness and good character never fade. Beauty alone will not make a husband to be pleased with his wife, what make a husband to be pleased with his wife is her righteousness, her good character and the service of fidelity. You may agree with me that some women are divorced; still they are beautiful, charming, gorgeous, and pretty. Why does that happen? Because, they failed to possesses the qualities that I mentioned above. Therefore, beautiful should not be a mandatory or compulsory quality to be sought when selecting a wife. Blessed is he who chooses the righteous one and enjoyment is yours, happiness is yours, repose is yours, marital security is yours and prosperity is yours, provided you cultivate a farm land that is fertile.

QUALITIES THAT SHOULD BE SOUGHT WHEN SELECTING A HUSBAND

Righteousness (Deen), and good character. Prophet Muhammad (SAW) said, if a man comes to you seeking your daughter in marriage, and you are satisfied with his deen and character, marry her to him if not disaster (fitnah) and harm will become rampant on the earth (at-Tirmithi). This is a golden advice given by (SAW) to the guardians of women to marry them to the men of religious (deen) and good character. Unfortunately, this golden advice has been over thrown by the guardians of women because they think deen and good character is inconsequential when giving out their daughters or sisters in marriage. What they take as an important factor to consider when giving out their daughters or sisters to a man in marriage is wealth, social status and prestige. It has reached a stage in our society today, when a man proposed to a woman for marriage the parents or guardians of the woman will investigate how much does the man earn per month, how much does he has in his bank account, which kind of car is he riding, which political position does he occupied in the society and is he well off (rich) or poor. If the answers to these irrelevant questions are negative, automatically the man is a poor candidate to them and they will not allow their daughter to marry him even though he has good

Islamic background and also have good character. This problem is not only restricted to the parents or guardians alone both girls too, they don't want to marry someone that is poor even though he has taqwa and good character. All they want is a man that is affluent even though the deen and good character is nowhere to be found. And that is the reason corruption has prevailed on the earth, fornication has increase due to high demand from the girls and their parents too because less privilege cannot afford to marry. Marriage has been failed because the purpose of the marriage was not based on Allah sake alone but for material things. Richness and wealth does not bring happiness and repose in marriage, what brings happiness and tranquility in marriage is righteousness and good character. Any relationship that is based on material things alone, the outcome (result) of that relationship is failure and the happiness and repose will not be there in their marriage. Well, I am not advocating that Muslim should dwell in poverty but my emphasis is that wealth, social status is peripheral or minor factors that should not be compared or exchanged with deen and good character. When someone is poor today does not mean that Allah will not enrich him tomorrow. Allah says; (marry those among you who are single and righteous of your male and female slaves. If they be poor, Allah will enrich them out of his bounty..... (Qur24:32). This is the promise of Allah that He will enrich them (needy). Therefore, wealth, social status and prestige should not be her major concern on whether or not to marry him, because when a woman marries a man that has deen and good character, he will always respect her and treat like a queen. Above all, his deen and good character will be a greatest opportunity for her and her children towards improving in their deen.

CHAPTER THREE

Benefits of making the right choice

There are a lot of benefits when you marry a right spouse. But the benefit will only be achieved when you follow the profound qualities that have been discussed in chapter two of this book when selecting a life partner.

1. You will have repose and happiness in your home
2. A believing woman will always help her husband in regard to the affairs of the hereafter.
3. She is a security guard upon herself and her husband property.
4. Always give you shoulder to learn on.
5. She is your special and personal advice in affairs of this dunya

Consequences of making the wrong choice

There is a lot of danger and hazards when you made a wrong choice in marriage.

1. When you marry a bad wife, response and happiness will not be there in your home even though you are rich, you will be frustrated and your home will be like hell.
2. Bad wife always push their husband to disobey Allah in order get their heart desire.
3. Her bad character will also affect the children because; children do inherit their mother's attitude.
4. Herself and your property are not in a save zone, anything can happen because she doesn't have God fearing (Taqwa).
5. Husbands do have setback in their lives due to their wives attitude.
6. Above all Allah does not answer some ones prayer that keeps a wife that has bad character in his house and refuse to divorce her.

CHAPTER FOUR

Istikharah (seeking Allah's guardians)

Before courting, is recommended to perform Istikharah first. "Istikharah is a supplication (dua) to Allah for seeking his guidance in forming a decision or choosing the proper course" Narrated by Jabir Ibn Abdullah (Rda) he said; the prophet Muhammad (SAW) would instruct us to pray for guidance in all of our concerns just as he would teach us a chapter from the Qur'an. Prophet Muhammad (SAW) would say "if any of you intends to undertake a matter then let him pray two supererogatory units (two rak'ah of nawafil, recite (Alfatiha and suratul Kafirun in the first raka'at. And then recite Alfatiha and suratul Iklas for the second raka'at. Reciting that surah is not compulsory) of pray and after which he should supplicate.

Allahumma inni astakhiruka bi'ilmika wa'astaqdiruka bi-qudratika, wa'asaluka minfadlikal azim, fa-innaka taqdiru wala'aqdir, wata'alamu wa-la a'alam, wa-anta'allamul-guyub. Allahuma in kunta ta'alamu anna hazal'amra (his need) khairun lifidini wa-maashi, waaqibati amri, faqdurhu li wayassirhu li thumma barikli fihi. Wa in kuntata'alamu anna hazal amra, sharrun lifidini wama'ashi, wa-aqibati amri, fasrifhu anni wasrifni anhu, thumma waqdirliyal khaira haithu kana ardinibihi.

Meaning of the Dua, "O Allah, I seek your counsel by your knowledge and by your power I seek strength and I ask you from your immense power, for verily you are able while I am not and verily you know while I do not and you are the knower of the unseen; O Allah, if you know this affair (mention your need) to be good for me in relation to my religion, my life, and end, then decree and facilitate it for me, and bless me with it, and if you know this affair to be ill for me towards my religion, my life and end, then remove it from me and remove me from it and decree for me what is good whenever it be and make me satisfied with such."

After you have performed your istikharah, the next step to take is seeking advice from trustworthy people because any one that seeks Allah guidance and consults the true believers never regret. Allah says; consult them in the affairs. Then when you have taken a decision, put your trust in Allah, certainly, Allah loves those who put their trust in him. (Qur'3:159)

Don't ever make deadly mistake to approach a woman (propose) without consulting Allah (i.e. performing istikharah), because a woman may appears to you very righteous and also having good character, whereas she is not. You may not know because, we humans beings we doesn't have the knowledge of unseen, but when you consult Allah by performing istikharah, if she has any bad omen (bad character) Allah will surely prevent you from marrying her. Those that consult Allah before undertake any affaires never regret and also those that work with sense never look senseless!

Courting in Islam

When a man found a girl (woman) with the qualities that we discussed in the chapter two of this book, then the next step for him to take is to propose to her. And the process of proposing to a woman is called courting. In this chapter, we will discuss courting that is permissible in Islam and courting that is not permissible in Islam, because most of the men do make mistakes when courting a lady. Some enter through doors, while others enter through windows and backyards as well to court a lady.

Permissible courting in Islam (door courting)

In ideal situation, when you see a woman that you love and also possess the qualities that we discussed in chapter two of this book, you don't have the right to talk to her or propose to her. You must meet her parents or her guardians first to seek their permission. If they give you the permission to talk to their daughter, Then you go ahead and propose to her (seeking her hands in marriage), but if they refused to give you the permission or the authority to talk her, then you don't have the right to propose to her. Going against their decision is haram in Islam.

The prophet Muhammad (SAW) asked Abu Bakar for A'isha hand in marriage. Abu Bakr said; "But I am your brother" the Prophet (SAW) said, "you are my brother in Allah religion and his Book, but she (A'ishah) is lawful for me to marry (Sahihi Al-Bukhari).

Furthermore, you can seek permission by yourself or you can send your parent or relatives and also friends to seek permission for you for her hand in marriage (is allowed in Islam).

Windows or backyard courting

Window or backyard courting, is a courting which a man approach a woman and propose to her without seeking permission from her parents or guardians. This kind of courting is not recommended in Islam and it should be avoided.

A woman can present herself for marriage to a righteous man: A woman can present herself for marriage to a righteous man. Narrated Thabit I was with Anas while daughter was present with him Anas said; a woman came to prophet Muhammad (SAW) and presented herself to him saying O (SAW), have you any need for me (i.e. would you like to marry me)?" There upon Anas daughter said, "what a shameless lady she was! Shame! Shame"! Anas said, "she was better than you; she had a liking for the prophet Muhammad (SAW) so she presented herself for marriage to him (Sahihi Al-Bukhari).Furthermore, a woman can send her parents or guardians to talk to a man she likes. By doing that is not a disgrace or degrading to her status moreover, is accepted in Islam. Therefore, is the duty of the parent to check whether the man issuitable to become her husband by using the formula given by our beloved prophet Muhammad (saw) which says whenever a man comes seeking your daughter's hand in marriage and you are satisfied with his deen and character then marry her to him.

It's permissible to look at a woman before marrying her: Prophet Muhammad (SAW) said; Go look at her: it will then be more possible to have harmony between the two of you. And prophet (SAW) also said; "when one of you courts a woman, it is permissible for him to look at her if he only look because he seeks to marry her even if she does not know (that he is watching her)" (Ahmad and Al-Tabarani).

Impermissible courting in Islam

1. **Courting or proposing to a woman that has already courted by another Muslim brother**

It is haram (Prohibited) to propose to a woman that has been courted by another Muslim brother (that is, to propose to a lady that is engaged) But one can wait till the first suitor marries her or leave her. Prophet Muhammad (SAW) Said; none should ask for the hand of a lady who is already engaged to his Muslim brother, but one should wait till the first suitor marries her or leaves her (Sahihi Al-Bukhari).

2. **courting a married woman**

Proposing to a married woman is haram (prohibited) in Islam. Prophet Muhammad (SAW) said; " He is not one of us who turn a woman against her husband or slave against his master". (Abu Dawud, Al-hakim). It is a great sin to court or having extra marital affairs with a married woman.

Warnings

Whenever your proposal is accepted does not authorized you to have sexual intercourse, kissing, hugging, romance or even touch her, because engagement is just a mere approval by her parents that is not binding until the final binding agreement is reached (marriage contract)." Some western ideologies has been employed by the Muslims during engagement process such as engagement ring and engagement party all of these are innovation (Bidi'ah) in Islam, it should be avoided because, it is the practice of disbelievers (Kufar) and does not have basis in Islam.

CHAPTER FIVE

FUNDAMENTAL PILLARS OF LOVE

This chapter is aimed to discuss some qualities that are the engine or soul of love and affection; they increase love and affection whenever they are present and also exterminate love whenever couples or lovers failed to possess those qualities. Constructing a solid love, the lovers must fulfill or possess some qualities that I will discuss below. Love is just like a construction work, client will not get what he want at the first day he engaged the contractor for the proposed project but by executing the project final stage will be reached. Likewise love, you may not get hundred percent what you want in a spouse at the first time you met her/him. What you need to do is that, you should check whether he/she possess the qualities that we discussed in chapter two of this book, if yes, then, you should proceed to build her the way you want her/him to look like. To achieve a strong and vibrant love and affection both parties (i.e. man and woman) must have these qualities which I termed as fundamental pillars of love.

Fundamental pillars of love and affection are:

1. Taqwa (piety):

It serves as a moderator, security guard and law enforcement agent and also adviser towards human behavior. Taqwa (piety) or God fearing is the internal guard that makes someone to abstain from saying or doing things that are forbidding by Allah. Therefore, any relationship that its foundation was laid on taqwa (piety), such relationship will not suffer from ill treatment such as cheating (committing adultery or fornication) and maltreatment because of the fear of Allah. Furthermore, to construct a solid and vibrant love and affection both parties must have this quality in their dictionaries. Whenever taqwa is lost you will be hearing cases of infidelity and maltreating.

2. Caring:

Caring is kind, concern, gentle, helpful, and sympathetic towards other people. Caring is the life and soul of love and also engine of affection. Any relationship that lacks caring attitude, automatically the love and affection will be dead. Whenever something bad or unpleasant happen to your spouse, always show concern and feels as if it is you that such thing happen to. Therefore, to build a solid love, both parties (man and woman) must possess caring attitude towards each other. It doesn't cost any penny to have caring attitude in your dictionary. Love keeps on existing when there is a care and disappeared when there is not.

i. Sympathy

Sympathy is one of the features of caring, sympathy "is a natural feelings of kindness and understanding that you have for someone who is experiencing something very unpleasant". When something bad happen to your lover always sympathize with him/her. And try to comfort him/her by giving him/her should to lean on.

ii. Help

Help is assistance giving to someone who is in need. Wise men said; "a friend in need is a friend in deed" so, always assist your lover when he/her is in need, don't wait till he/she ask for it. Always be a good observant.

iii. Gentleness

Gentleness is another features of caring. We should always be gentle to our spouses and also avoid being harsh to them.

3. Truthfulness:

A truthful person does not lie and always says what is right (truth) even though it will cost him injury or loss of property.

Truthfulness is an essential quality that both parties (lovers) should all possess in their relationship. When the spouse observed that they are fair to each other and always telling each other truth, it brings about trust in their relationship and when trust is present love and affection do increase rapidly. But in a relationship where truth doesn't exist, they always lie to each other, the outcome of their actions will be harmful to their relationship because it will destroy trust, and when trust has been destroyed, it will result to hatred. And when hatred emanate in their relationship, automatically it will affect the love and there will not be peace in their home. Prophet Muhammad (SAW) said; "indeed, truthfulness leads to righteousness, and righteousness leads to jannah. Indeed, a man would continue to practice and pursue

truthfulness until he is recorded with Allah as a most truthful. And indeed, lying leads to immorality, and immorality leads to fire. Indeed, a man would continue to practice and pursue lying until he is recorded as a liar" (al-Bukhari and Muslim).
Therefore, we should always say the truth, don't think that if you tell your partner what you did, he/she will be angry, of course, he/she will be. It is better to tell your spouse the truth than concealing it from him/her. Because when the truth reveal itself the outcome will be bad. But when you tell your spouse the truth, he/she will be angry and the outcome of his/her anger will be less when you apologize, then to allow the truth to reveal itself. To build a solid love and affection, we should be truthful to each other because it's our truthfulness that will vindicate us from any trouble.

4. Respect
Respect is one of engine of any successful relationship. Respect is admiration that you show to someone because of his/her good character or social status, "respect is reciprocal" when you respect people, they will surely respect you too. To build a solid and vibrant love, lover must respect each other. Any relationship that lacks respect, the outcome will be bad. It doesn't cost anything to be respectful to others, therefore, be respectful and achieve your optimum goals.

5. Forgiveness
Forgiveness is another vital quality that both lovers should always have in their dictionary. All human beings are fallible. We all have our shortcomings in life. Some people think that when you are in love with someone, you will not do something's that will hurt them or make them apoplectic. I said this is a wrong perception for those that believe that. Father and son have misunderstanding and also wrong each other let alone husband and wife. Therefore, mistake is inevitable in any relationship. Prophet Muhammad (SAW) said; "he who does not show mercy, no mercy will be shown to him by Allah. And he who does not forgive will not be forgiven" (Ahmad and at-Tabarani). Therefore, our beloved prophet Muhammad (SAW) never revenge whenever he is wronged unless you touch Allah. He is our role model and we should emulate him (SAW) in our day to day activities. Lovers that possess high level of maturity are those that

forgive each other without taking revenge.

6. Apology

Apology is another essential quality that couples should also have in their dictionary. "Apology is a statement that tells someone that you are sorry for doing something wrong or for causing a problem". This is where major problem lies; some people are so arrogant up to an extent that they can't even apologize for doing something wrong. They felt that why should they apologize to someone which is not even up to their level or social status. Prophet Muhammad (SAW) Said; anybody that has arrogant that is equivalent to a weight of an atom; he/she will never enter paradise. Apology is a tool that mitigates apoplexy to the lowest level. It doesn't cost anything to say, I am sorry my love please forgive me.

Lastly, it's not recommended to fall in love with someone that is arrogant because their will not be a humility in that relationship and their matrimonial home will be like a hell. Sometimes you have to apologize to your lover not that you are wrong but for peace to reign. Happiness and joy is he/she that always tender apology.

7. Fair hearing

Fair hearing is an opportunity giving to a person by a court of law to give the reason of his actions before passing a judgment on him. In other words, is a way of giving a convicted person to give his own side of the story in order for a court to know whether he is guilty or not. Fair hearing is right giving to humanity in order to avoid exploitation and was originated from the Qur'an. Allah says, and (remember) when we said to the angels, prostrate to Adam" so they prostrated except Iblis (Satan). (Qur'18:50). Allah gives the command to all angels that they should prostrate to Adam and they all prostrated but Satan refused to prostrate. Allah knows the reason why Satan (Iblis) refused to prostrate but Allah give the Satan the opportunity of fair hearing by asking him.

Allah said; O Iblis (Satan); what prevent you from prostrating yourself to one whom I have created with both my hands. Are you to proud (to fall prostrate to Adam) or are you one of the high exalted?" and Iblis (Satan) Said; I am better than he, you created me from fire, and you created him from clay." And Allah says them get out from here, for verily, you outcast and verily, my curse is on you till the day of recompense (Qur. 38:75-78). As we can see from above ayat (verses), before Allah passes his judgment on Satan (Iblis), Allah asked Satan first not that he (Allah) doesn't know what stopped him (Satan) from prostrating, but Allah gave Satan the opportunity of fair hearing before passing his judgment on him. In another verse, when the two angels came to prophet Dawud in form of human beings. They entered in upon Dawud he was terrified of them, they said; "fear not! We are two litigants, one of whom has wronged the other, therefore judge between us with truth, and treat us not with injustice, and guide us to the right way.

Verity, this brother (in religion) has ninety nine ewes while I have only one ewe, and he says "Hand it over to me, and he overpowered me in speech.

Prophet Dawud said; immediately without listening to the opponent (the second party) "he has wronged you in demanding ewe in addition to his ewes. And verily, many partners oppress one another except those who believe and do righteous good deeds, and they are few". And Dawud guessed that we have tried him and he sought forgiveness of his Lord and he fell down prostrate and turned (to Allah) in repentance (Qur' 38:22 – 24).

Therefore, what I want to infer here from the above verses (ayat) is that, prophet Dawud seek forgiveness of his Lord because he passed judgment without listening to the second party. To build a solid love, lovers must give their partners room for fair hearing before passing their judgment on them. Don't ever judge someone based on your intuition or feelings, always try to give a listening ear for your lover to express himself before taking any action.

Benefit of fair hearing

1. It enables the arbitrator to give a valid verdict.
2. It eliminates suspicious as well as giving room for dialogue.
3. It gives access for mutual understanding between the partners. Everybody should be entitle to this privilege before passing judgment on them

8. **Trust**

Trust is another essential pillar of love, which lovers should also have in their dictionary. When someone feels his/her partner is reliable, honest and fair in their dealings, it creates a trust in one's heart. And whenever there is trust in any relationship, that relationship will flourish in happiness and joy because they have confidence in each other. And there will not be anything like suspicious which will hinder the growth of love and affection in their hearts. Lovers should always avoid suspicious because is the tool that Satan (Iblis) used to create ill feelings in their hearts. Whenever there is an ill thought or bad feelings against each other, it destroyed the loves and affection that exist in the heart. Allah says; O you who believe avoid much suspicious, indeed some suspicious are sins (Qur 48:12). And Prophet Muhammad (SAW) said; beware of suspicious for suspicious is the worst of false tales (Al-bukair.) As we can see from above verse and hadith of (SAW), suspicious is a sin and Allah and his messenger says we should avoid it because suspicious is the worst of false tales. Lovers should always avoid judging their partner based on what they are suspecting from their partner or base on their feelings. When you want to judge your partner it should be based on facts and genuine reasons, because that is the only way to figure out the truth and to eliminate suspicious and ill feelings. Lovers should always trust each other's for betterment of their relationship.

9. **Silence**

Silence is a medicinal tool that can be used in any relationship to solve some problems or to mitigate apoplexy. Silence is consequential tool that lovers should have in their dictionary. One of the Islamic scholar said; "he never quarrel or fight his wife, likewise his wife too. And their marriage was thirty something years old. People were astonished with such testimony, and they asked him how did they achieve that? He said; whenever my wife is angry, I kept quiet (silent) without altering a word and whenever I am angry too she kept quiet." We can observe from the above testimony that silence is a vaccine to some matrimonial problems. We should always learn how to be quiet even though we are right in order to avoid problems in our matrimonial homes. Wise men said; "the best answer to the airhead is silence." Silence does promote peace in relationship; when you observed that your partner is fed up with you; don't retaliate by becoming mad too. You should always keep quiet and don't prove to him/her that you are temperamental too for peace to reign.

10. Accolade

Accolade is "an expression of praise and admiration for someone" this quality do increase love and affection. Whenever your partner did something in order for you to be happy even though you don't like it, always admire it and praise him/her for his/her effort. This is the only way that will make your partner to improve and also put more effort in performing his/her duties in order to make you happy. Always praise your partner by telling him/her, honey you are best. Partner that doesn't receive eulogy always become reluctant when discharging their duties. Therefore, it doesn't cost anything to tell your partner that you are the best.

11. Gratitude

Gratitude is vital quality that does increase love and affection. Unfortunately, most of the women are ingrate to their husbands which lead to destruction in their matrimonial home indirectly. Gratitude is an act of showing your appreciation to someone for what they have done to you or what they have given to you. Most women lacks this quality and are ungrateful to their husband most of the time that is why Prophet Muhammad (SAW) said; the major dweller of hell is women because they frequently are ungrateful to their husbands (Bukhari &Muslim). And in another hadith (SAW) said; he who is not grateful to men is not grateful to Allah. We can see the danger of being ungrateful to someone or your partner, we should always be grateful to our partners in order to build strong and vibrant matrimonial homes. It doesn't cost anything to say honey I am grateful (thank you, so much my love).

12. Understanding

It's a very vital quality that lovers should also have in their encyclopedia. They should try to understand each other feelings and weaknesses, because it will give them good insight on how to put up with each other behaviors. To construct a solid love, lovers must understand each other very well. Everlasting love and affection does not build it selves, and also it's not built in a day. It requires a lot of effort, time and passion to build it. Whenever lovers fulfill the above criterion discussed above, I guarantee you strong and everlasting love and affection (Insha Allah). It doesn't cost any penny to have these qualities that have been discussed above in your dictionary. Those that want already made things always get the opposite but "Determination, hardworking, persistence, perseverance and prayer lead to success".

CHAPTER SIX

DUTIES OF SPOUSES

I decided to share some light on this topic, duty of spouses in order to give all the unmarried men and women good insight on what is accepted (duties) from couples to fulfill in their matrimonial homes. It is very essential when you want to venture into any contract, you oath to know your duties thatis obligatory on you to fulfill in order to achieve the stated goals.

The major problem couples are facing nowadays is that, most of the couples (husband and wife), doesn't know their duties that is obligatory upon them to fulfill in their matrimonial home and that is the reason why some marriage contract has failed and also some matrimonial home been broken into pieces.

Therefore, in this chapter, we will discuss duties that couples have to fulfill in order to construct strong and happy home. Marriage is all about negotiation.

Negotiation is a process were people come together to discuss and reach an agreement in order to achieve a specific goal.Likewise, marriage too, couples come together and agree to live together for the rest of their lives in order to achieved specific goal too. Therefore, this goal or objective will not be achieved unless the couples fulfil their duties.

DUTIES OF HUSBAND

Prophet Muhammad (SAW) said; "have taqwa of Allah in regard to your woman. Indeed, you took them in marriage through a trust with Allah, and had access to their private parts by Allah' word (permission). They have a right on you that you provide them with food and clothing in a fitting manner" (Sahihi-muslim). Allah says; men are in charge of women because Allah has made one of them to excel the other and because they spend to support them from their wealth (Qur' 3:34).

1. Provision of basic needs

Husband must provide basic needs for his wife such as food, clothes and shelter.

As we can see from verseand hadith mentioned above, the primary duties of husband is to provide food, shelter and cloth for his wife and provision of these basic things will be based on the husband capacity, because Allah says; Let the rich man spend according to his means, and the man whose resources are restricted, let him spend according to what Allah has given him, Allah puts no burdenon any person beyond what he has given him, Allah will grant after hardship, ease. (Qur'65:7). As we can see from the above Qur'an verse, man will only spend or provide basic things such as food, cloth and shelter according to his power (i.e. What he can afford) pushing him to do what is beyond his power is a great sin; and automatically you (wife) are disobeying Allah, because Allah says he should spend according to his means (Source of income). This does not mean that men should be parsimonious. Rich should spend according to his power without reducing anything because it is a command of Allah.

2. Protection

Man (husband) must protect his wife because Allah says. Men are in charge of women (Qur' 3:43)

Protection can be categorized into two

Protection in deen (religion)

Physical protection

Protection in deen (religion);Man (husband) must make sure that his wife have piety (taqwa) by guiding her toward observing her compulsory Ibadatsuch as five daily prayers, fasting, charity and also make sure she engage herself in some Ibadat such as (Nawafil Fasting, prayer, recitation of Qur'an and so on). Allah says; O you who believe ward from yourself and your families a fire (hell). (Qur' 66:6). This is a command given by Allah, that men (husbands) should protect themselves and their families (wife and children) from fire (hell). To protect your family from hell you have to make sure that they fulfil the promise of their Lord (Allah), that they will worship none but Allah alone and also make sure that, you (husband) doesn't feed your family with haram (prohibited) things, only from halal source (right source). To achieve this, you and your family must have taqwa (piety). That is the reason why is recommended by prophet Muhammad (SAW), that a woman should be giving to a man in marriage who has taqwa and good character. Because a man that doesn't have taqwa (God fearing), he doesn't care if his wife is righteous or not and he will be feeding them with haram things which will both lead them to hell. "Prophet Muhammad (SAW) said, a man is a guardian of his family and responsible for them (Sahihi-Bukhari)".

i. Physical protection

Physical and emotional protection is very vital in life, husband should make sure that his wife is protected from any physical and emotional hazard, and also make sure that the environment is conducive for his wife which will enable her to discharge her duty by performance.

3. Al-ghaira (self – respect, honor)

Sa'ad bin Ubaida said; "if I saw a man with my wife, I would strike him with the sharp edge of the sword" the Prophet Muhammad (saw) said to his companions, "are you astonished by Sa'ad (Ghaira) sense of honor? By Allah I have a greater sense of Ghaira then he has, and Allah has still greater sense of Ghaira than I have" (SahihiBukhar). In another hadith, prophet Muhammad (SAW) said; person that doesn't have sense of protection or honor towards his wife will never enter paradise (Jannah). Having sense of protection or honor towards your wife, is what make her to feel that you truly love her and by doing so, you are following the Sunnah of (SAW).Unfortunately, most of the men lack this quality in their encyclopedia, they allowed their wives to chat or display their beauty to men that are not their maharram which is haram in Islam. That is why, some dreadful sin such sexual harassment has increased because men lack self-respect towards their wives. Prophet Muhammad (SAW) said; addayuth (person that doesn't have sense of Ghaira) will never enter paradise (Jannah). Addayuth is a filthy person that thinks he is civilized whereas he is not, we Muslim our civilization should be based on Qur'an and Sunnah of (SAW) not coping or emulating some westerners as our role model.

Allah Says; indeed, in the messenger of Allah (SAW) you have a good example to follow for him who hopes in the meeting with Allah and the last day and remember Allah much (Qur'33:21). Blessed is he who knows the purpose of his creation.

4. Help

Husband (man) should always assist his wife in doing or carryout some home activities such as washing dishes, clothes, cooking and sweeping. Some men think that helping his wife doing such home activities is shameful and degrading to their honor and dignity. They will say, why will I do such kind of activities, I my a woman? Nay, they don't know that is what prophet (SAW) used to do when he is Indoor. A Suhaba ask our Mother (Aisha) "what did the (SAW) did at home? She said; "he used to be at the service of his family; and when it was time for prayer, he would go out to pray" in another narration, "he act like order men, he will mend his cloths, milk his goat, and serve his self" (Bukhar, Ahmad).As a man you have to show good example in your home not just by leading or talking but by performing the job too.

5. Fulfilling your wife sexual desire

This is another vital role which man (husband) must fulfill. A wife has an ample right upon her husband for emotional feeling and physical satisfaction.

Prophet Muhammad (SAW) said; "O Abdullah have I not been informed that you fast all the day and stand in salat (Prayer) all night"? I said, yes O Allah's messenger this "He said do not do that observe the saum (fast) some times and also leave the saum (Fast) sometimes and stand up for the salat (Prayer) at night and also sleep at night. Your body has a right on you, your eyes have a right over you, you and your wife have a right over you." (Sahihi Bukhari)

Therefore, this duty must be accomplished or fulfilled by the husband.

6. Kind, gentle and polite to the women

Prophet Muhammad (SAW) Said, "I command you to take care of

the women in a good manner for they a create from a rib and the must crooked portion of the rib is its upper part, if you try to straighten it, you will break it and if you live it, it will remain crooked, so I command you to take care of the women in a good manner". (Sahihi Al-Bukhari).

This hadith is telling us to understand the fragile nature of women. In another hadith prophet Muhammad (SAW) said, "the best of you are those who are best to his family, and I am the best of you toward my family". (Al-trimithi, Ibn Hibban). We should always be kind and gentle with our wives, we will surely enjoy them.

13. Law abiding (Discipline)

As a man (husband) you have to be law abiding in your house. You don't expect your wife to follow your rule and regulation set by you, whereby, you don't used to conform with those rules too. We should always be law abiding citizen in any where we find ourselves.

DUTIES OF WIFE

As you know that, men (husbands) have some duties to fulfill in order to make conducive home for his partner. Likewise, their wives have some duties to accomplish too in order to make their matrimonial home conducive for both of them. Allah says; men are the protectors and maintenance of women, because Allah has made one of them to excel the other, and because they spend to support them from their means. Therefore the righteous women are devoutly obedient to Allah and to their husbands, and guarding the husband's absence what Allah orders them guard (i.e. their chastity, their husband property) (Qur8:34).

As we can see from above verse (ayat), women have to fulfill some duties too in order to make their home habitable for living.

1. Submission

From the above verses (ayat), a righteous women, are women who are obedient to Allah and to their husband, and a woman cannot be obedient until she is submissive to Allah command and to her husband will too. Allah said; he made a man to excel them (women) because they spend to support them from their means (wealth). This authority given to men by Allah should not be challenge or disputed by women. And whenever a woman is obedient to her husband automatically she is obeying her creator (Allah) and when she deplored her husband, automatically she has deplored Allah too.

Prophet Muhammad (SAW) said; "were I to order a person to prostrate before another person, I would have ordered the woman to prostrate before her husband" (Al-Tirmithi and Ahmad). In another narration (SAW) said; If woman knew her husband prerogative (right), she would not sit while he is eating his dinner or super until he finishes eating." (Al-Tabaran).

In another narration too (SAW) "A husband right upon his wife is such that if he had an ulcer and she licked it for him, she would not fulfill his right by that" (al-Hakim).

The above hadith emphasizes the great prerogative of the husband upon his wife. From the above hadiths, we observed that women cannot fulfill their husband rights (100%) but what is required from her is obedient toward her husband orders and also to serve her husband to the best of her abilities, which involve doing or performing some daily activities in her matrimonial home with optimum professionalism which will attract her husband's attention. A woman can only serves her husband properly when she is obedient to him. Unfortunately, some women are arrogant to the extent that they don't have obedient in their encyclopedia. They think they have become sophisticated, no man can rule or control them as he want. They forgot that for them to have taqwa (piety), they must be submissive and obedient to their husband rules and regulation. Subjecting yourself to your husband, doesn't mean that he is better than you in the sight of Allah but you are fulfilling the commandment of Allah and his messenger (SAW) by obeying him. And remember that this authority or power that he has over you, he wasn't the one that gave himself but Allah and his messenger (SAW) gave it to him. If you want to earn the pleasure of your Lord (Allah) and also dwell in joy and happiness in your matrimonial home always be submissive and obedient to your husband. Prophet Muhammad (SAW) said; when a woman prays her five daily prayer, fast in the month of Ramadan, preserve her chastity, obeys her husband she will be told on the day of judgment enter Jannah from eight gate (Ibn Hibban)

2. Guardian

We observed from the aforementioned verse (ayat) that, another duty of righteous women in their husbands houses is that, they are guards in their husbands houses what Allah orders them to guard such as their chastity and their husband property. Prophet Muhammad (SAW) said; a wife is a guardian of her husband's house and she is responsible for it. (Sahihi Al-Bukhari).

A righteous woman never give her body to another man, she safeguard her chastity even though her husband is away from home and she will never misuse or dispose her husband property without his consent. And also never spend lavishly from her husband property.

Prophet Muhammad (SAW) said; when a woman prays her five prayer, fast the month of Ramadan, preserves her charity and obeys her husband, she will be told on the day of judgment "enter jannah from any of its eight gates" (ibn Hibbar), woman should be good guardian in their home because they will surely give account of their actions.

3. Fulfilling her husband sexual desires

One of the greatest aim or objective of marriage is to avoid zina (fornication) because Allah says; don't come near to the unlawful sexual intercourse, verily, it is a fahishah (great sin) and evil way that lead one to hell. (Qur'17:32) this is the warning of Almighty Allah that we should not commit illegal sexual intercourse. Therefore, the only way for someone to maintain his/her chastity is by marriage, which is the only way a spouse can vent out his/her sexual desire legally. This is a great responsibility upon women to willingly at any time to assist their husband to relief themselves from tension. It is a great sin for a woman to deny her husband bed.

Prophet Muhammad (SAW) Said; "By the one that Muhammad's soul is in his hand, a woman would not truly fulfill the right of her lord (Allah) until she fulfils all of her husband's right even if he was to ask her for herself while she is in a camel's saddle, she should not deny him that" (Ahmad, ibn Majah).

Prophet Muhammad (SAW) Said; if a man invite his wife to sleep with him and she refuse to come to him, and then the angels sends their curses on her till morning (Sahihi-Bukhari). Therefore, women (wives) should make themselves available at any time when their husbands seeks to have intimacy with them in order to avoid been cursed by the angels of Allah.

4. Permission

A righteous and respectful woman (wife) always takes permission from her husband before doing anything. Don't ever leave your matrimonial home without his permission or embarking in any affairs without seeking his endorsement. Wise women are those that admitted their husbands to become the head of the family and become their necks, if the neck does not move, how will the head moves.

6. Sympathy, Help and Kindness

These are vital qualities that a wife should possess or have in her dictionary, these qualities has been discussed in chapter two of this book under the fundamental pillars of love.

COUPLES SHOULD AVOID THE FOLLOWINGS

1. **Insult**

Don't ever insult your life partner. Whenever he/she made a mistake, correct him/her but not insult. Always remember that human beings are all fallible, we learn better from our mistakes. Furthermore, Prophet Muhammad (SAW) forbids insult, vulgar and obscene words or spurious statement.

2. **Fouls Language**

We should avoid fouls language; if you don't have anything better to say always learn how to keep quiet. Prophet Muhammad (SAW) said; if you cannot speak truth or good please be silent.

3. **Argument**

Always avoid argument with your spouse's because sometimes argument doesn't yield any positive things.

4. **Suspicious**

We should always avoid suspicious because it destroy trust. Never judge someone without valid or genuine reasons or facts, suspicious has been discussed in chapter five of this book under the pillars of love.

5. **Ugliness**

Don't ever tell your life partner that he/she is ugly even though he/she is. He/she will be unhappy and the worst part of it is that he/she will never forget such word that you altered to him/her. Avoid such word even though you are playing or joking and never called her with a name that she doesn't like.

6. **Aggressiveness**

Psychologists says "aggressiveness is a symptom of madness" why will you employ madness into your home or your relationship? Avoid being aggressive because it destroys home and relationship. What patient does not give aggressive will not give it to you.

7. **Conditional love**

Conditional love is a love that is based on some material things such as money. A girl will say to a man that before showing him, her love, he must give her money or buy some materials for her. Avoid such kind of love because it doesn't go anywhere, if you want to love, love because Allah and if you want to hate, hate because of Allah.

8. Ungrateful

Always show appreciations to your lover, being ingrate to your partner exterminate love and affection of your partner and also make your husband to hesitate when doing something. He will feel reluctant to buy things for you, because you don't show appreciation at all. Always show your gratitude to your life partner, not only your spouse but those that deserve it.

9. Laziness

Laziness is another bad attitude that exterminates love. When the couples are lazy automatically their relationship will be bore. None of them is ready or willing to construct the strong and everlasting love and affection. And love is just like a construction of structure. You will never get hundred percent what you want in a wife or husband but the best solution is that you will build your spouse the way you want her/him to look like. When the couples are ready to work they will be able to construct a strong and vibrant love and affection within a short period of time by mutual agreement and hardworking.

When you marry someone that is lazy no one will tell you how your home will look like.

10. Happiness or sadness

Don't display joy when your partner is worried neither display sadness when your partner is happy, by doing so, it will hatch hatred.

11. Dirtiness

Always make sure that your body is free from impurity (Dirty), your home is clean, your clothes are washed and iron. Avoid dirtiness in your home and also odors too. Always used perfume in your home to delete some stinking things

12. Divulge

Never reveal your spouse's secret to any outsider because it is dangerous to the well-being of your matrimonial home, and that was the reason prophet Ibrahim (ASW) told his son prophet Ismail to divorce his wife because she was unable to conceal the secret of her husband. And Prophet Muhammad (saw) forbid that. Never be a blabbermouth.

13. Voluntary Ibadat without permission

Woman should not fast (voluntary) and also admit people in her husband house without his permission. Prophet Muhammad (SAW) Said; "it is not permissible for a woman to fast, while her husband is present without his permission except Ramadan. Nor is it permissible for her to admit any one to his house except with his permission" (Al-Bukhari, and Muslim).

14. Conversation with non Maharam

Women should avoid having conversation with men that are not their maharams and also they should avoid seclusion with men.

15. Smiling

Women should avoid smiling with men that are not their maharams because smiling gives access for further exploitation, and they should also avoid displaying their beauties in public.

16. Outdoor type

A good woman should always avoid going outside unnecessarily, most especially without her husband permission. Allah says; stay in your houses do not display yourselves like that of the time of ignorance (Que'33:33)

.

17. Nagging

Couples should always avoid nagging. Nagging does not yield any positive outcome but open door for Satan to manifest in your relationship. Learn how to forgive and forget.

18. Too much demanding

This is one of the attribute of women which some of them have being born with. Asking your husband to do this, buy that. This kind of attitude make some husband (men) to avoid coming home early because they know that when they are present their wives will never allow them to rest. They will prefer to hang around. Women should avoid this kind of attitude of demanding much from their husband they should manage the little which their husband provide for them. Women should be economist in their matrimonial home not spending lavishly.

19. Miser

This is one of the attribute of men. Men doesn't like spending their money, they prefer storing them. ''Hind bint utbah came to prophet Muhammad (SAW) and said; indeed my husband Abu Safyan is a parsimony (miser), he doesn't give us what will suffice me and my children, unless what I take without his awareness, prophet Muhammad (SAW) Said; take from his wealth what will be enough for you and your children. (SahihiMuslim).

This hadith of Prophet Muhammad (SAW) does not give or permit women to steal their husband's money or wealth, this rule is only applicable for a man that is stingy (miser). Men should avoid being stingy or parsimonious (miser), is not a good character at all.

20. Never harm your husband

Prophet Muhammad(SAW) Said; "whenever a woman harms her righteous husband in this world (Dunya) his future wife from paradise (Jannah) will say," Do not harm him, may Allah fight you, he is only staying temporarily with you, and will soon come to us" (Ahmad)

We observed from the above hadith that any woman that harms her righteous husband in this world, his future wives in paradise will curse her. Please women should avoid harming their husband.

21. Avoid beating

Men should avoid beating or hitting their wives, most especially their faces. Allah says; as to those women on whose part you see ill conduct, admonish them (fist), next, refuse to share their bed and last beat them (Qur'4:34).

The first solution giving by Allah is that when you notice ill-conduct of your wife, you admonish her by dialogue. You can involve her family members to serves as reconciliation team between you and your wife.

Second solution is that you can refuse to share her bed (avoid having sex) with her for a while, perhaps she will change her attitudes; the last resort is to beat her. It's recommended to avoid beating in some occasions; beating doesn't yield positive result sometimes. Furthermore, our beloved prophet Muhammad (SAW) never beat his wives even ones. We all know that sometimes our mothers did annoy him. Why can't we emulate him?

22. Neglecting your family

"Prophet Muhammad (SAW) said; "a sufficient sin for you would be that you hold (support) of those whom you are responsible for feeding (Sahihi-Muslim)." It is a great sin to neglect those that you know that you are their bread winner, never neglect you responsibilities.

23. Displeasing Allah

Women should avoid disobeying Allah in order to please their husband. Whenever your husband commands you to do something that is prohibited (haram) by Allah and his messenger, you don't have to obey him. "prophet Muhammad (SAW) Said; obedience may not be offered to a human being if it involves disobeying Allah, obedience should be in good thing" (Sahihi-Al-Bukhari and Muslim).

24. Don't keep malice

Couples should avoid keeping malice with their lovers; because keeping malice with someone in Islam is prohibited (haram). Keeping malice will not mitigate or solve the problem. Whenever conflicts arise, always learn how to solve or mitigate it amicably not by keeping malice.

25. Illicit sexual intercourse (Zina)

A true believer will never commit adultery or fornicate because it is a great and dreadful sin. Allah says; don't ever come near to the unlawful sexual intercourse verily it is a great sin (Fahishai) and an evil way that lead one to hell (Qur'17:32). Righteous couples never commit adultery or fornicate, they vent out their sexual desire in a lawful way. Men should always rush to their wives to vent out their sexual desire in a lawful way in order to avoid committing illicit sexual intercourse (zina) and likewise women too. Adultery exterminates marriage and it should be avoided.

THINGS THAT ARE RECOMMENDED FOR COUPLES TO DO IN THEIR HOMES

1. Entertaining your wife

You should always entertain your wife by playing with her, telling her stories that will make her happy and also brings joy to her heart. Don't ever make your home like a soldier barrack. We should always play with them, because this was the practice of our beloved prophet (SAW), He do plays with his wives too.

2. Nick name

Give your spouse a sweet nick name such as Baby, Sweetheart, Darling, Honey, My love, my heart, my life, my apple, sweetie, my own etc. Such kind of names have great impact in a relationship, is a mistake to call your spouse with his/her real name.

3. Pronouncing your love to your spouse:

Always pronounce your love to your spouse by telling him/her I love you, whenever you have a conversation with your spouse on cell phone, before ending the call tell him/her, baby I love you, before going out as a man always tell your wife, honey I love you and she should always replied with I love you too not only thank you. Pronouncement of love is a medicine to some matrimonial problems. Therefore, pronouncement of love should be always not occasionally.

4. Pray for each other:

Spouse should always pray for their love ones whenever your husband prepares to leave home for in search of livelihood, always pray for him. Firstly, hold his hands before you pray and the prayer should be in this format. O Allah, protect my husband for me from the evil of devil the outcast, protect him from the evil of the jinn kind, O Allah protect him from the evil of mankind. O Allah grant him his wishes, O Allah put Baraka in his Endeavour, O Allah I place his safety in your hands, return him for me safely and healthy amen. Finally, you should say to him, my love, always avoid haram (Prohibited) things, I love you. When he went out the pray will keep on ringing in his mind and it will increase the love and affection in his heart. Anytime that is signing some files in his office, Wallahi, he will keep on remembering you because of the Dua (prayer) that you made for him.

5. False cry:

It's recommended for a woman to pretend as if she is crying whenever her husband wants to leave home for in search of their livelihood. She can even shed tears. When you cry, definitely your husband will ask you, baby why are you crying; the answer should be in this format. My love, whenever you leave home, I do miss you a lot and I want to be with you always, I don't want to spend any minute or second without seeing your face or feeling your presence. When you replied him in this way, Wallahi, something will stirred in his heart that, my wife truly loves me, and it will increase the love and affection that he has for you and when he leaves home his mind will not be at rest till he is back. This is the best way for a woman to set a trap for a man to fall in, by loving her much and Allah will surely reward her.

6. Adornment:

This is another critical aspect that women should not joke with because it has great impact in their relationship. Women are expected to keep their (body) clean, they should always bath at least three time in a day, keep their matrimonial home clean, and they should make sure that everywhere is tidy and also wear clothes that are prepossessing. They should not display their adornment for anyone to see but only their husband, don't allow your husband to smell or perceive some bad odor coming out from you or see you in a dirty mood. Always make sure that you are clean and neat and also apply some perfume too and likewise men too.

7. Welcoming your husband:

Some women do not know how to welcome their husbands which is a great problem to them. This is the best format to follow in order to give him an official welcoming. First, when your husband says Assalamu alaikum, you should also reply with salaam too, rush to him greet him and hug him. After that, hold his hand, tell him how much you missed him and also say Alhamdulillah, Allah has brought you back safely and healthy for me, I am happy. After that, let him know that he is now in his house not his office by giving him a hot kiss. After that, take him to bathroom and bath him, after taken his bath you now serve him his food by feeding him. This is an official welcoming for lovers. It does create a strong bond between you and your husband; because he would say my wife truly cares for me.

8. Eat together:
It is recommended that lovers should always eat together because (SAW) do eat with his wives.

9. Bathing together:
It is also recommended to bath with your wife because is a Sunnah of our beloved prophet Muhammad (SAW), he do bath with his wife. Bathing with your wife create a strong bond between you and your wife. In addition to this, women should always comb their husband bears and hair and also rub cream on their body after taken their bath and also give your husband cloth that you want him to wear.

10. Cook:
Cooking is another vital responsibility of women in their husband house and it should not be taken for granted because it has a great impact in any marriage. Unfortunately must of the women nowadays, doesn't know how to cook a delicious food, they prefer wasting their precious time on social network chatting and streaming videos. A woman that doesn't know how to cook, it's a great problem that can affect her relationship with her husband because her husband will always be teed off when he eats her food. But a woman that know how to cook very well, whenever her husband eat her food he will be happy even though he was slightly angry with her. Therefore, women should learn how to cook a delicious food.

11. Washing and polishing:
A good wife always makes sure that her husband clothes are clean. She will wash her husband's clothes; iron them without waiting for her husband to tell her to do so. Dedicate yourself toward serving your husband and he will be your servant.

12. Looking at the good side of your wife.
Allah says; live with them honorably if you dislike them, it may be that you dislikes thing and ALLAH brings through it a great deal of good (Qur4:15), and prophet Muhammad (SAW) said; let not a believing man hates a believing woman, if he dislike one of her traits, he would be pleased by others" (SahihMuslim). This verse and Hadith mentioned above shows that we cannot get hundred percent

what we (men) want from them (women), they have lapses and the best thing to do is to overlook those lapses and move ahead.

13. Have a leisure time with your family

Always create a special time for your family. It shouldn't be from work to work, from Calabar to Abuja, from Lagos to Kaduna, you don't have time for your wife at all. It's bad because it has a negative impact in her life, she will always feel lonely and depressed, but when you always spend time with her, she will feel happy and comfortable. Always spend time with her, teaching her Qur'an and hadith and other Islamic books if you are capable to do so but if you are not, you should enroll her in Islamic school.

14. The best charity is feeding your family

Prophet Muhammad (saw) said; "a money that you spend for Allah's sake (jihad), a money that you spend to free a slave, a money that you give as a charity to needy, and a money that you spend on your family: the one that has a great reward is that which you spend on your family (SahihMuslim). We should always spend for our families in order to earn a greatest reward; we shouldn't be parsimonious towards our families.

15. Flatter your wife appearance

Man should always tell his wife that she is the best from the rest. I have never in my life seen any beautiful, gorgeous, elegance, charming and prepossessing woman like you. By saying that, she will feel happy even though she is not beautiful because you appreciate her appearance and she will try to upgrade and also rebrand herselffor you. And you should also say my honey you are the best cook I have ever seen in my life. Whenever you flattered her like that, even though she is not good in cooking, she will try harder to upgrade her cooking skills too. Women like praises, whenever you flattered them you will surely get more from them.

16. Motivation

Men should always motivate their wives either by giving them gift or award. Motivation has a great impact in any relationship, when you motivate your wife it will energize her to put more effort toward maintaining you and your children which will result to increment in love and affection. Motivation is not limited to giving money or gift but also kind words too.

17. Vital or essential activities that should be performed by the couples

Couples should always indulge in activities such as; sex, kissing, romancing, foreplays and hugging each other because such activities do increase love and affection. Such activities shouldn't be avoided unnecessarily, because those activities have a great impact in their marriage.

18. Hospitality

Women are expected to be kind and generous towards their husband's families and relatives too. Hospitality has great impact in your relationship too.

19. Admonition

Couples should always advice each other in a sincere and honest way in order to achieve their marital goal. Whenever you want to embark in any affair, always seek advice from your life partner before venture into it. It is a great mistake to embark on any affair without seeking advice from your life partner, if anything bad should happen to you who will you tell. Prophet Muhammad (SAW) used to seeks advice from his companions. Couples shouldn't hesitate from advising each other and also give each other a sincere advice that will yield a positive result.

20. Correction

Couples should always correct one another whenever they made mistakes. Mistakes are inevitable, because human beings are all fallible nobody is infallible. Whenever you want to correct your life partner, do it with hikmah (methodology) not with insults, vulgar or by shouting at your partner. Some people do make a dreadful mistake by ignoring correction, they will says, I will not correct my partner now but when I marry her/him I will correct some of his/her behaviors'. My people say; you cannot straighten a dry tree or wood. Correction is done as soon as the mistake has been made; use low tone and hikmah whenever you want to make correction because truth is bitter.

21. Entrepreneurial skills in love

Couples should be entrepreneurs in their relationship. What I mean is that, spouses should learn how to rebrand their love by employing new ideas in their relationship so that it will increase the love and affection that they have for each other. For instance, whenever you want to say honey I love you, then pronounce it with tajweed and whenever you want to talk to your life partner, do it in honorific way.

CHAPTER SEVEN

SPOUSES SHOULD DO THE RIGHT THING

The major problem that make some relationships to fail, marriage been broken or shattered and also couples living like a cat and dog that is, not living in peace and harmony. The reason is that the foundation of their marriage or relationship was laid on patient alone. In my own little research; I observed that most of the couples are not living in happiness, some that cannot put up with each other's attitude they go for divorce. While some are there living together as husband and wife because of their children or one thing or the other. According to oxford dictionary, patience is the ability to stay calm and accept a delay or something annoying without complaining. You may agree with me that patience has an elastic limit, that is, it has a limit in which someone can persevere or exercise patient, when the limit is exceeded it will result to apoplexy or retaliation because someone will no longer put up with such kind of behavior. Most at time the sermon given to the newly wedded couples is that, they should be patient with each other's. The parents or guardians will be telling them (bridegroom and bride) that for any relationship or marriage to flourish patience must be employed all the time, whenever patience is absent the marriage will fail. But for me I discarded this sermon because whenever a foundation of any relationship or marriage is laid on patience alone the outcome of that relationship is failure because patience has elastic limit. Therefore, foundation of any relationship or marriage should be laid based on doing the right thing. Couples should know their duty that is obligatory on each one of them to discharge by performance. Any relationship or marriage whose foundation is laid on this formula DO THE RIGHT THING, it will be difficult to see such kind of relationships or marriage suffering from ill treatment because the wife knows what she will do that will pleased her husband and also avoid things that will make him unhappy , likewise the husband too. They will always do things that will brings happiness to their matrimonial home and also avoid things that will shatter their matrimonial home. Couples can build a mini paradise in this world provided they discharge their duties by performance.

CONCLUSION

The critical condition in man's life is the transition stage when a man decided to have a life partner (wife), this stage is critical because it has a great and direct impact to him in this dunya and hereafter and also his unborn children to come either positively or negatively. If there is a stage in man's life that need ample time to make a proper decision, use professional skills, work hard and also pray hard in order to achieve his goal then, is the time that man's want a life partner (wife). The only help someone can offer to himself in this dunya, is to marry a good wife that will assist him in his religion and worldly affairs and that will also help him in raising righteous children. Scrutinize the land that you want to cultivate otherwise; you would get the opposite because whenever you plant in a land that is not fertile, it will affect the growth of the crops as well as affecting the yield too. Some scholars says, if you want to see the picture of your unborn children, then look at the woman that you want to marry". We shouldn't be carried away by physical appearance and worldly things. Physical appearance and worldly things alone does not bring happiness and repose in one's life and it doesn't increase love and affection. Therefore, success is paramount to us, but we cannot succeed in making a right choice (selecting a spouse) till we abide or follow the teachings of Islam. This book has provided some profound qualities that one should sought when selecting a life partner in order to dwell in happiness and joy and those qualities shouldn't be taking for granted. Lovers must make sure that they both implement those pillars of love in order to keep their relationship moving, because love dies whenever those fundamental pillars of love are nowhere to be found. Lastly, marriage is all about negotiation, couples (husband and wife) must all discharge their duties by performance that is binding on them without omitting any. Whenever a couple omit a duty intentionally that is binding on him/her to discharge, automatically it will lead to a problem. Lastly, couples must all discharge their duties by performance and also avoid things that will cause skirmishes in their marriage or matrimonial home.

ALHAMDULILLAH.

SOURCES

1. QUR'AN AND SUNNAH
2. ISHRAT UN-NISA
3. ADAB UZ-ZIFAFIL FIS-SUNNATIL MUTAHHARAH

www.ingramcontent.com/pod-product-compliance
Lightning Source LLC
LaVergne TN
LVHW041254150826
845673LV00008B/2584
* 9 7 9 8 3 7 1 6 3 1 9 8 5 *